Mel Bay and Alfred Publications Present...

Brazilian
Jazz Guitar

Chord Solos and Comping Etude for Each Song
Lead Sheets Included * Lyrics Included * Online Audio Recording

Arranged by Mike Christiansen & John Zaradin

Online Audio

To Access the Online Audio Go To:
www.melbay.com/WMB010MEB

1 2 3 4 5 6 7 8 9 0

Visit us on the Web at www.melbay.com — E-mail us at email@melbay.com

ONLINE AUDIO

Table of Contents

Introduction

Mel Bay Publications, Inc. and Alfred Publications are happy to publish this collection of Brazilian music arranged by Mike Christiansen and John Zaradin for guitar. Because two arrangers were united in this collection, the nomenclature reflects the thought process of each artist. In some cases the fundamental chord may be listed rather than the exact embellishment. Also, chord placement may vary. Some of the chords symbols in the lead sheet may be placed over beat one in a measure when the chord is actually sounding on the second half of beat four in some of the arrangements. Guitarists should analyze these arrangements and compare them to the original lead sheets to learn how the arrangers approached their pieces. These are the quintessential pieces from the Brazilian songbook. The arrangements will give any guitarist hours of pleasure from both practicing and performing this wonderful music.

A Day in the Life of a Fool

Bossa Nova

words by Carl Sigman
music by Luiz Bonfa

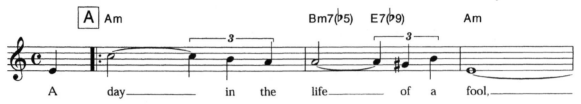

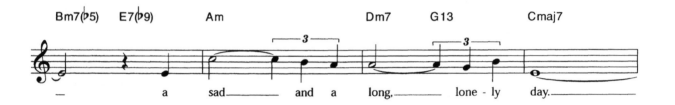

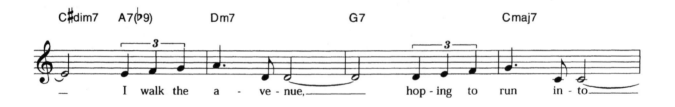

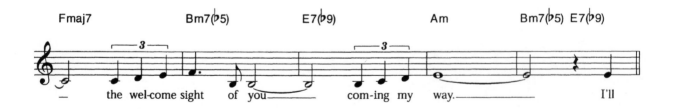

B

Am | Bm7(♭5) E7(♭9) | Am | Bm7(♭5) E7 Em7(♭5)

stop____ just a - cross____ from your door,____ but you're__ nev - er

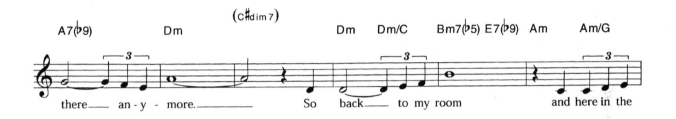

A7(♭9) | Dm | (C♯dim7) | Dm Dm/C | Bm7(♭5) E7(♭9) Am Am/G

there__ an - y - more.____ So back__ to my room and here in the

F13(♯11)
Fmaj7 | Bm7(♭5) E7 | Am | 1. Bm7(♭5) E7(♭9) | 2.

gloom I cry____ tears of good - bye.____ A — 'Til you

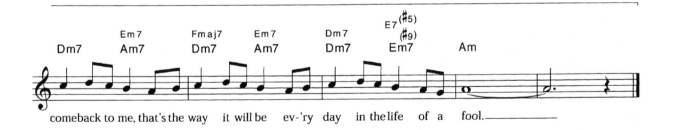

| Dm7 | Em7 Am7 | Fmaj7 Dm7 | Em7 Am7 | Dm7 Dm7 | E7(♯5)(♯9) Em7 | Am |

comeback to me, that's the way it will be ev-'ry day in the life of a fool.____

A Day in the Life of a Fool

(solo guitar)

arr. Mike Christiansen

words by Carl Sigman
music by Luiz Bonfa

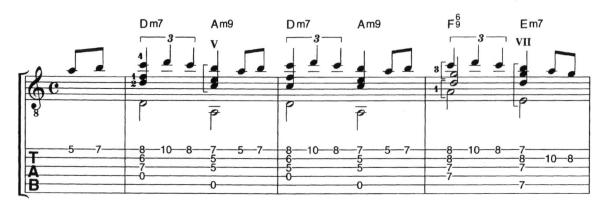

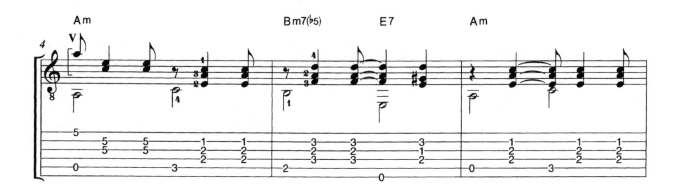

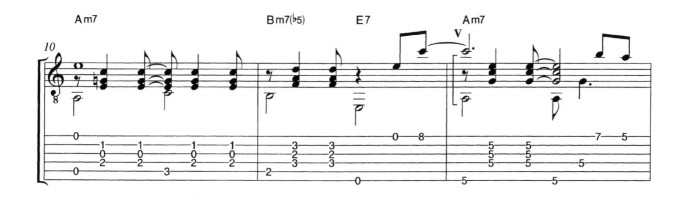

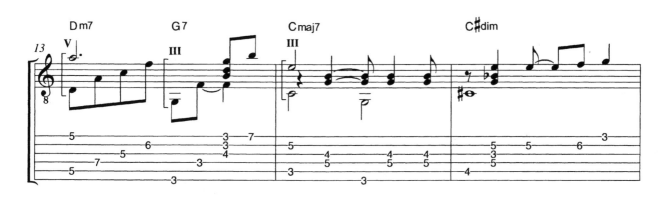

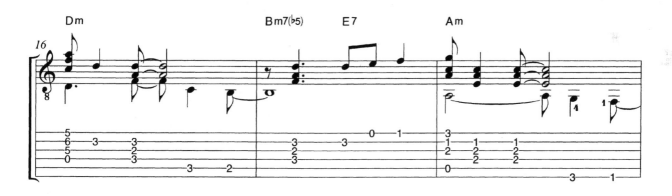

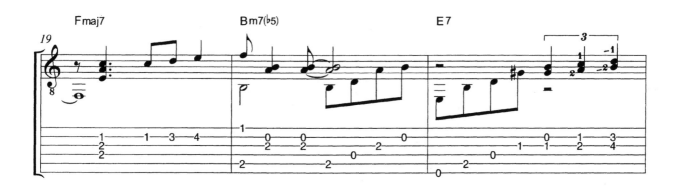

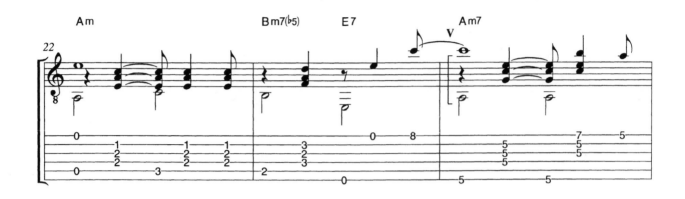

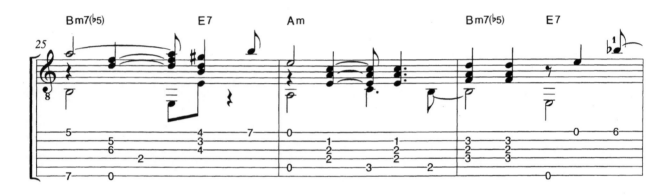

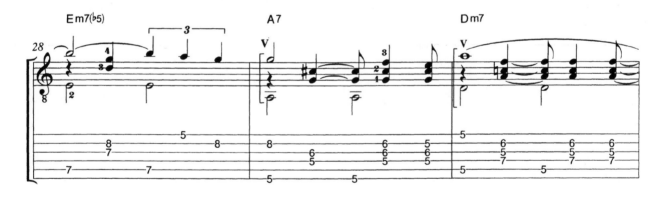

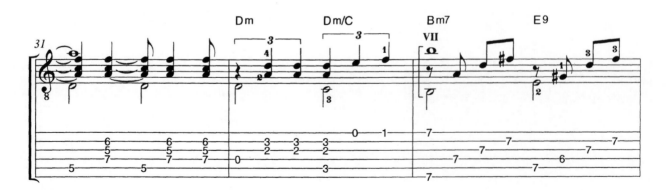

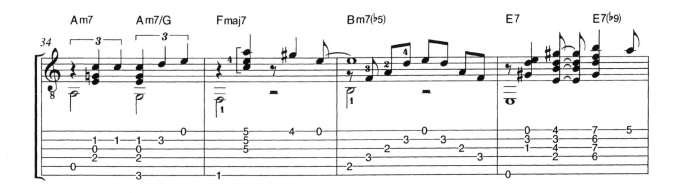

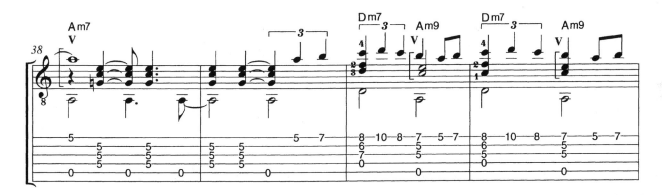

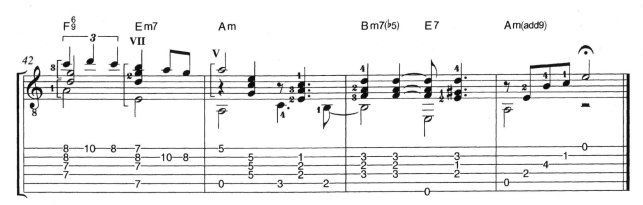

A Day in the Life of a Fool

(rhythm accomp. study)

arr. Mike Christiansen

words by Carl Sigman
music by Luiz Bonfa

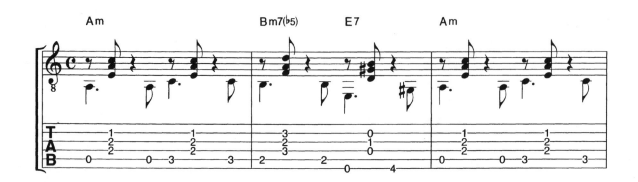

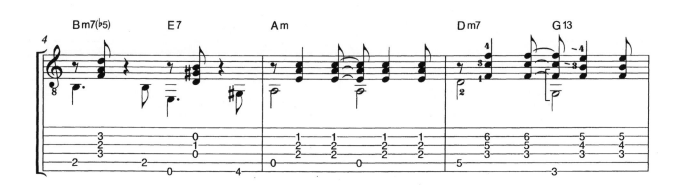

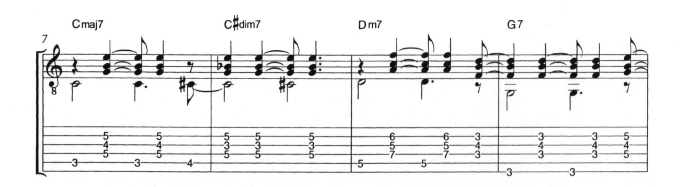

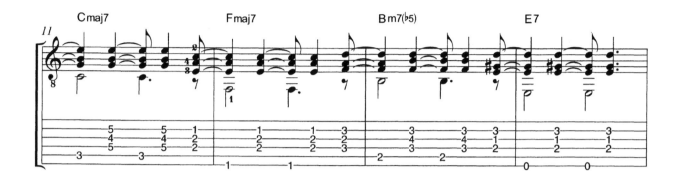

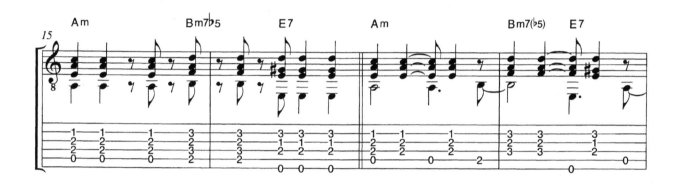

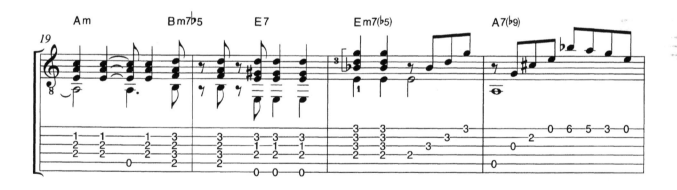

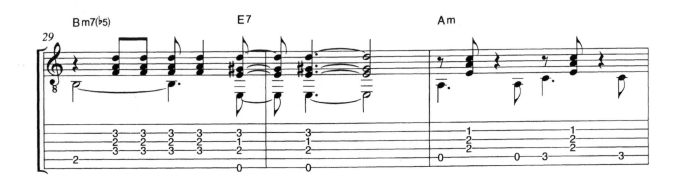

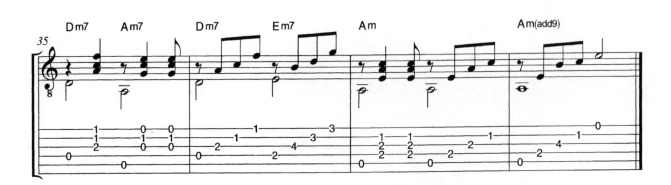

14

Chega de Saudade

(No More Blues)

original text by Vinicius De Moraes
music by Antonio Carlos Jobim
English lyric by Jon Hendricks and Jessie Cavanaugh

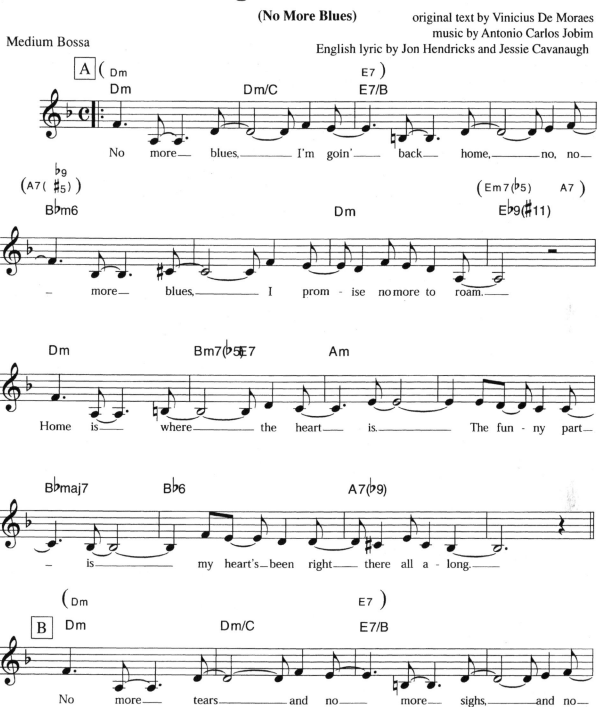

more fears, I'll say no more good - byes. If trav - el beck -

ons me I swear I'm gon - na re - fuse. I'm gon - na set -

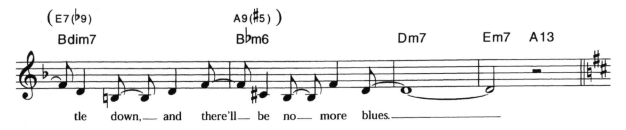

tle down, and there'll be no more blues.

C

Ev' - ry day while I am far a - way my thoughts turn home-

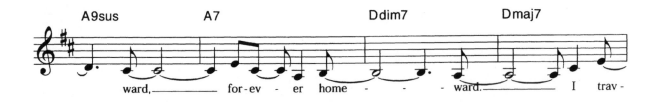

ward, for - ev - er home - - - ward. I trav -

elled 'round the world in search of hap - pi - ness, but all my hap -

Chega de Saudade

No More Tears

(solo guitar)

original text by Vinicius De Moraes
music by Antonio Carlos Jobim
English lyric by Jon Hendricks and Jessie Cavanaugh

arr. Mike Christiansen

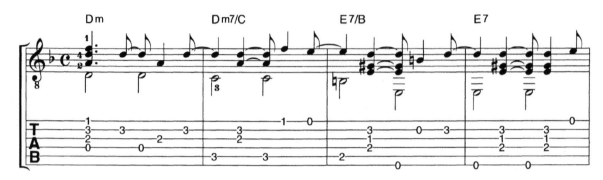

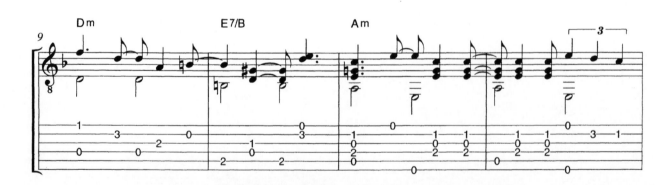

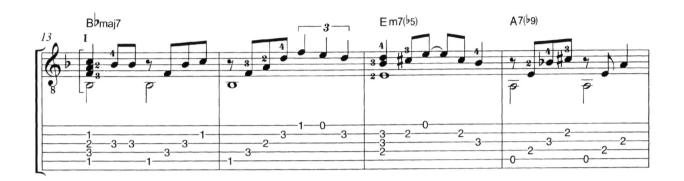

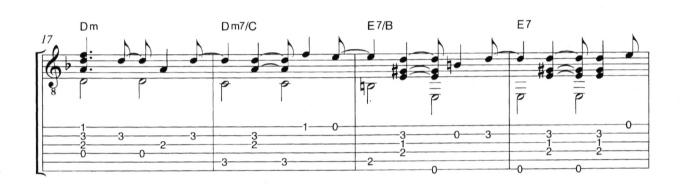

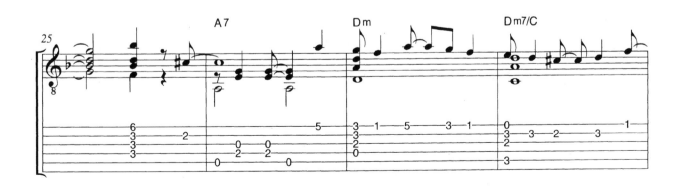

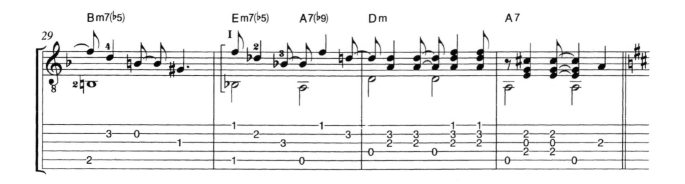

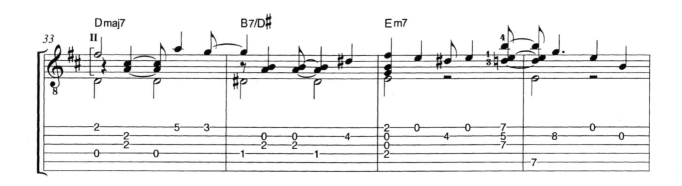

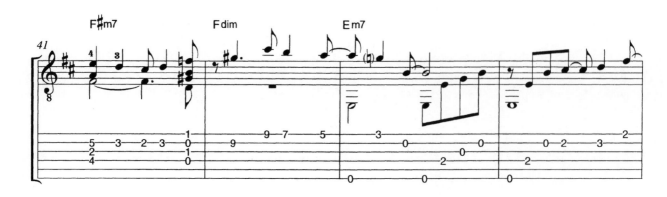

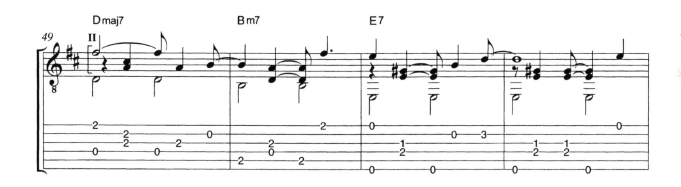

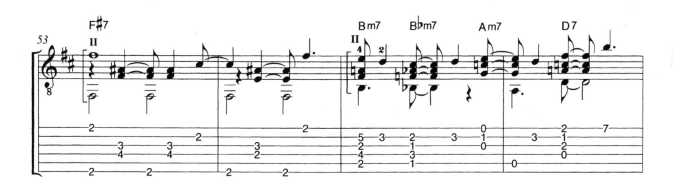

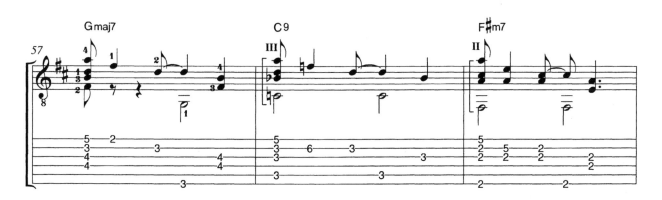

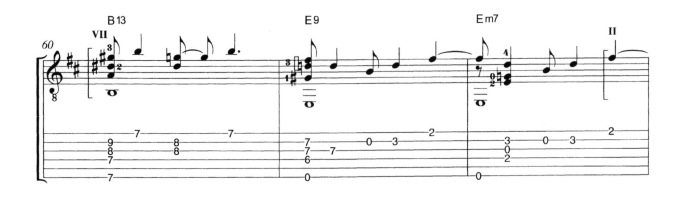

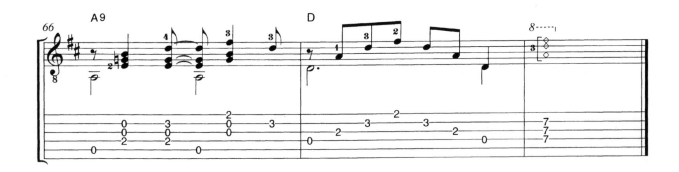

Chega de Saudade

No More Tears

(rhythm accomp. study)

original text by Vinicius De Moraes
music by Antonio Carlos Jobim
English lyric by Jon Hendricks and Jessie Cavanaugh

arr. Mike Christiansen

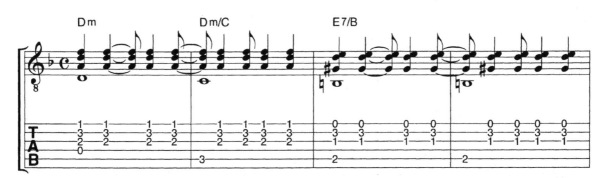

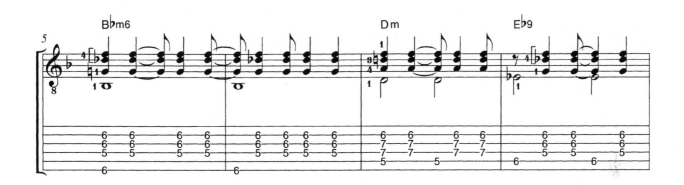

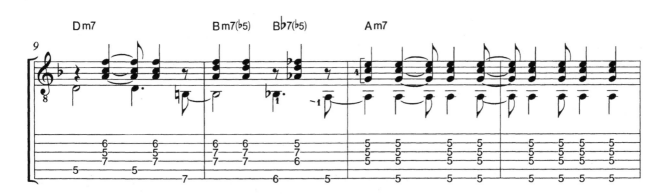

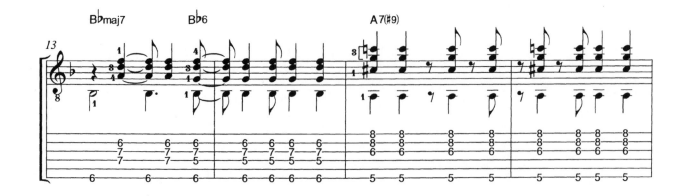

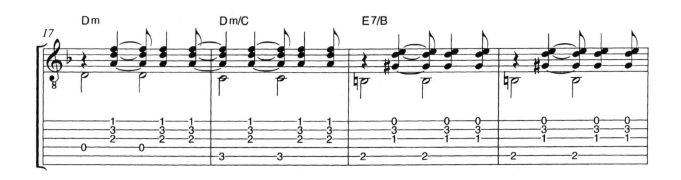

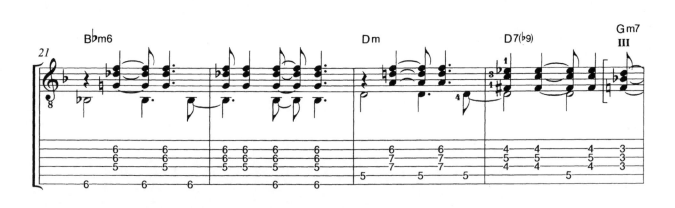

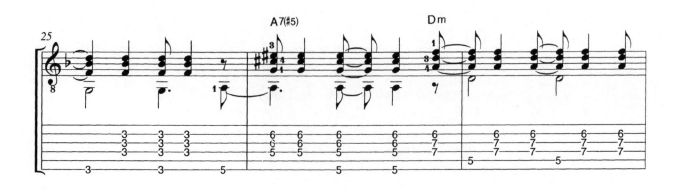

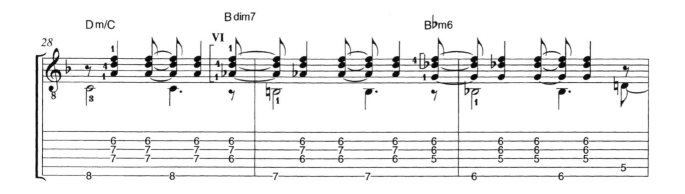

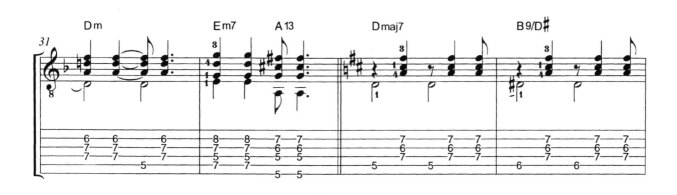

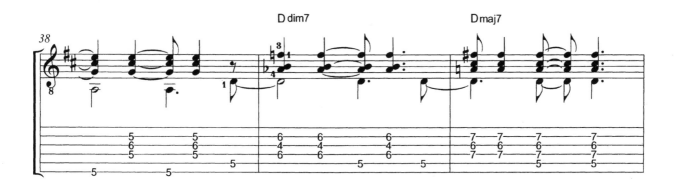

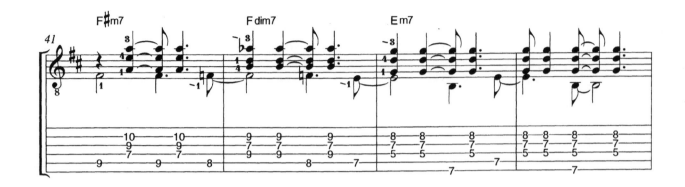

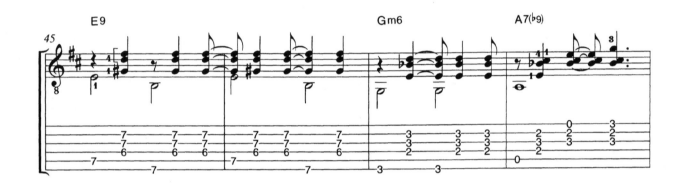

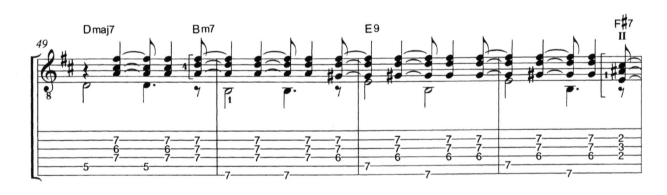

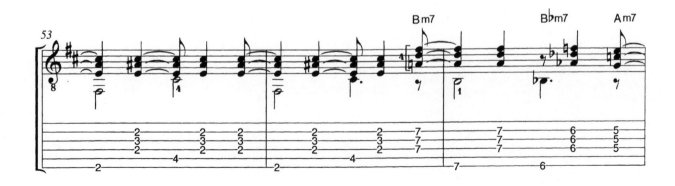

26

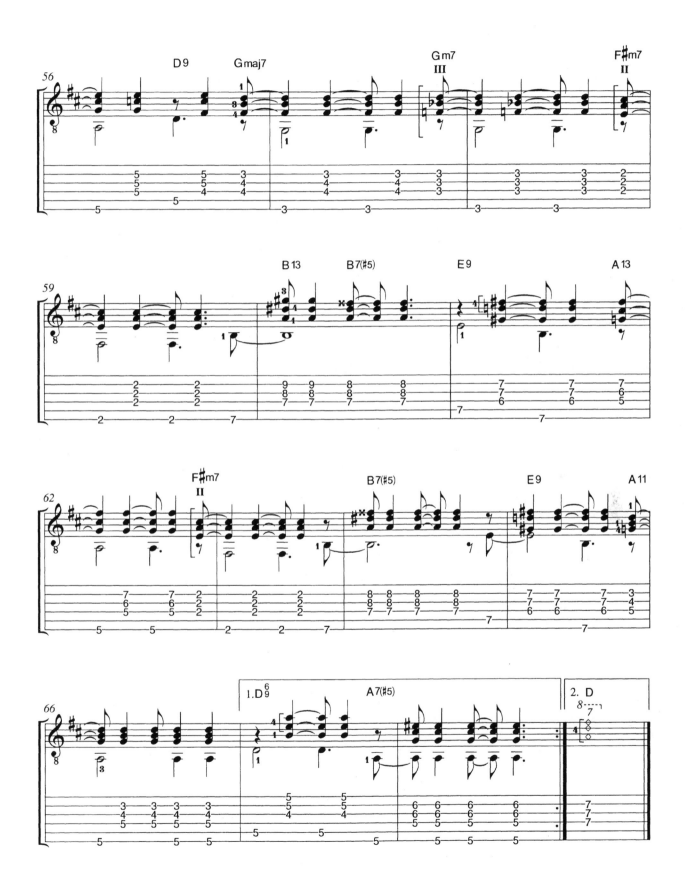

Desafinado

Medium Bossa

words by Jon Hendricks & Jessie Cavanaugh
music by Antonio Carlos Jobim

Love is like a nev - er end - ing mel - o - dy,

po - ets have com - pared it to a sym - pho - ny,

a sym-pho-ny con-duc - ted by the light - ing of the moon,

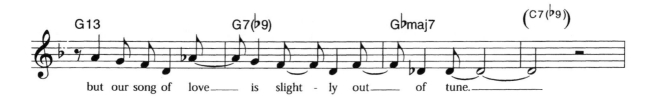

but our song of love is slight - ly out of tune.

Once your kiss-es raised me to a fe - ver pitch,

now the or-ches-tra - tion does - n't seem so rich,

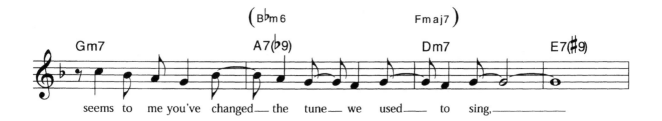

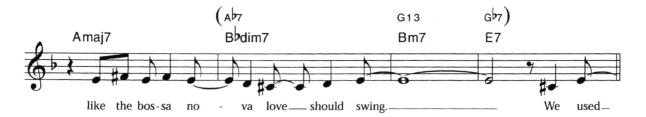

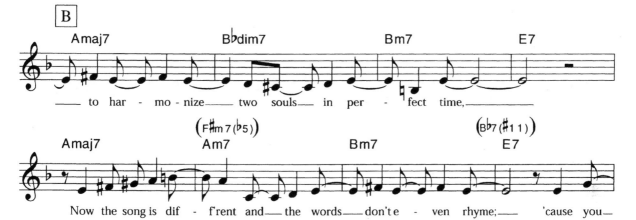

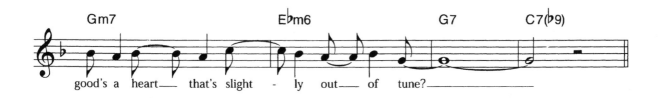

This page has been left blank
to avoid awkward page turns.

Desafinado
(solo guitar)

arr. John Zaradin

words by Jon Hendricks & Jessie Cavanaugh
music by Antonio Carlos Jobim

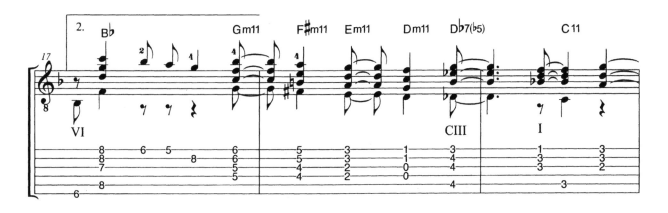

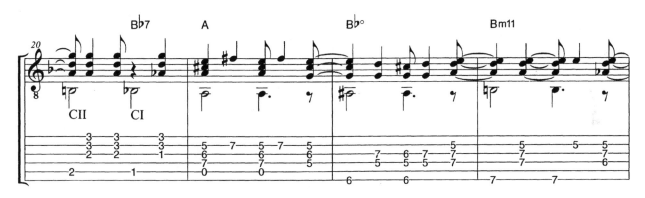

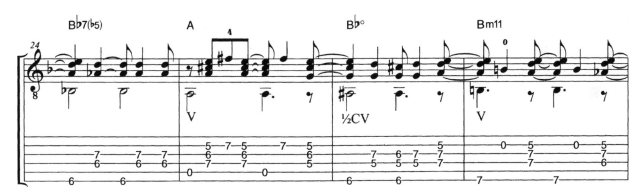

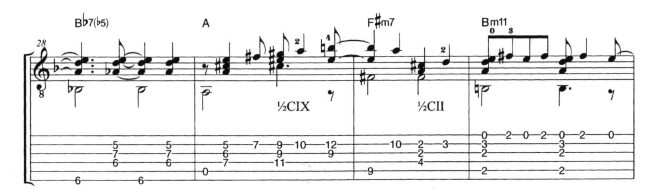

33

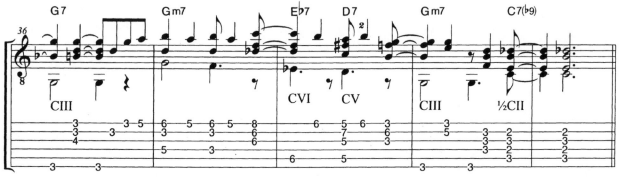

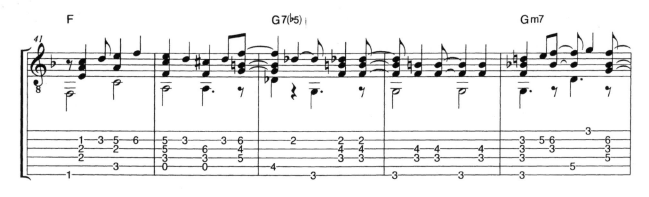

Desafinado

(rhythm accomp. study)

arr. John Zaradin

words by Jon Hendricks & Jessie Cavanaugh
music by Antonio Carlos Jobim

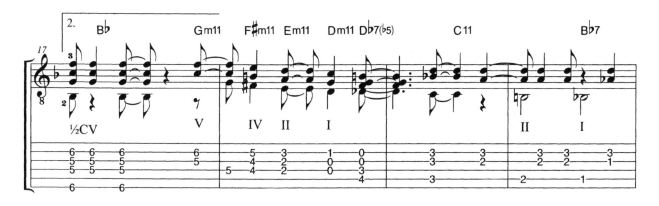

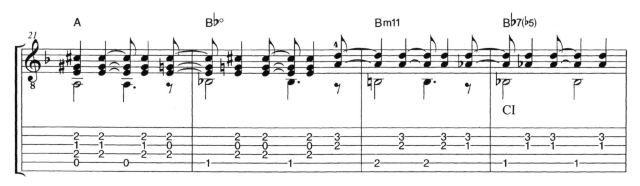

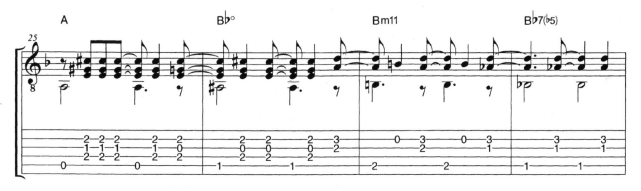

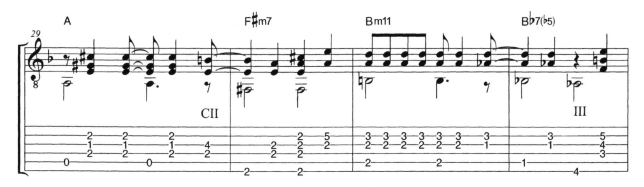

A Felicidade

(a/k/a Adieu Tristesse)

Meduim Bossa / Samba

words and music by Vinicuis De Moraes,
Andre Salvet, and Antonio Carlos Jobim

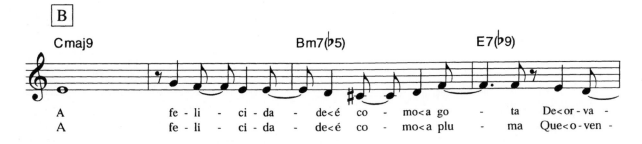

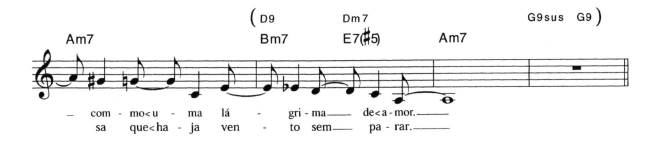

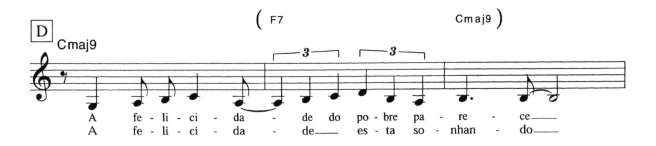

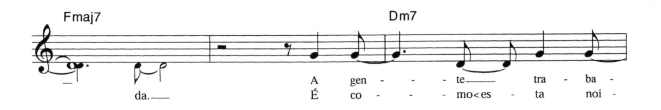

um mo - men - to de so - nho Pra fa - zer a fan - ta - si -
bus - ca da ma - dru - ga - da Fa - lem bai - xo por___ fa - vor___

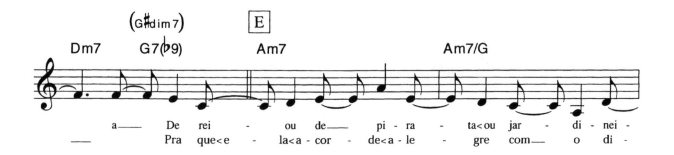

a___ De rei - ou de___ pi - ra - ta<ou jar - di - nei -
___ Pra que<e - la<a - cor - de<a - le - gre com___ o di -

ra. Pra tu - do se<a - ca - bar -
ra. O - fe - re - cen - do bei -

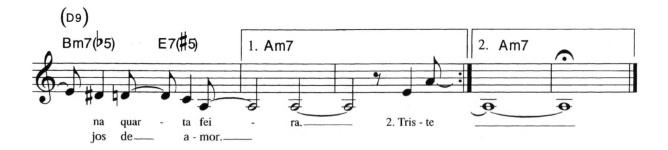

na quar - ta fei - ra.___ 2. Tris - te
jos de___ a - mor.___

42

This page has been left blank
to avoid awkward page turns.

A Felicidade

(solo guitar)

arr. John Zaradin

words and music by
Vinicius De Moraes, Andre Salvet,
Antonio Carlos Jobim

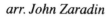

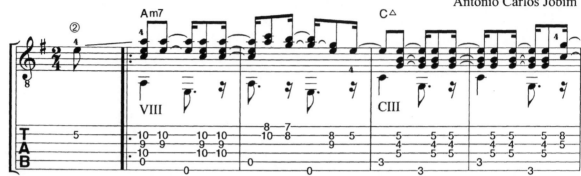

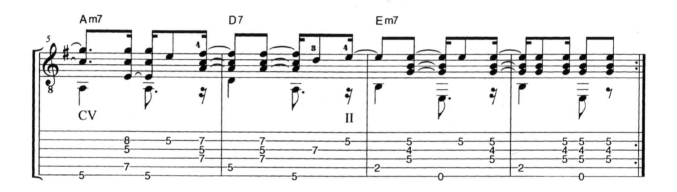

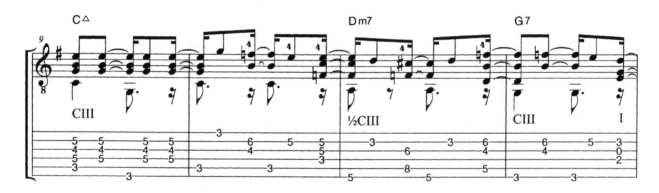

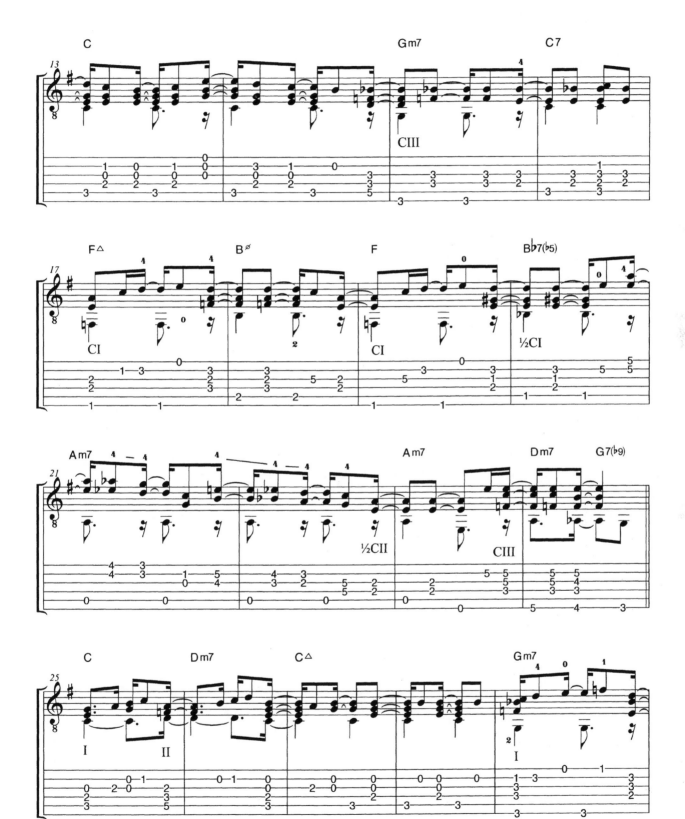

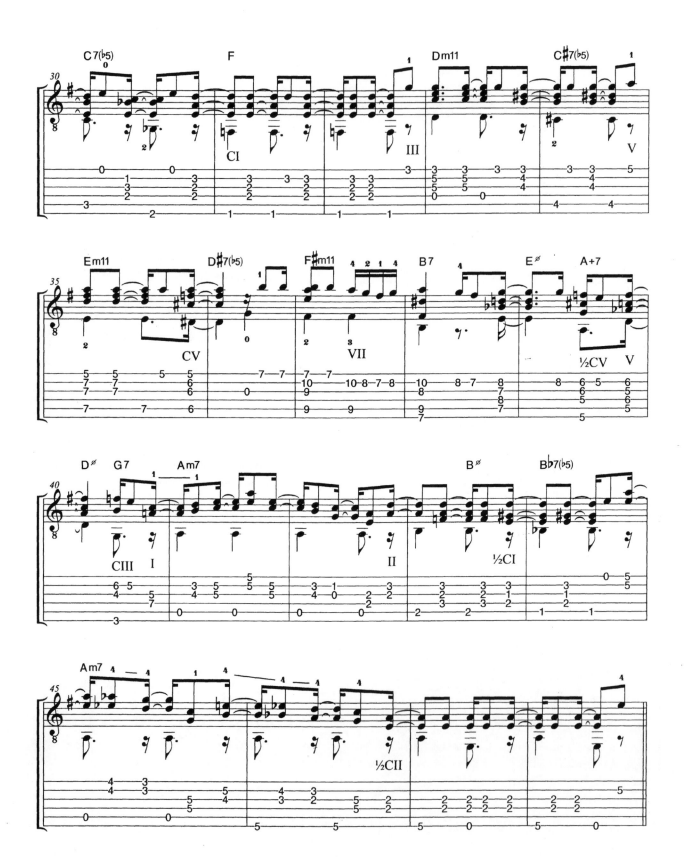

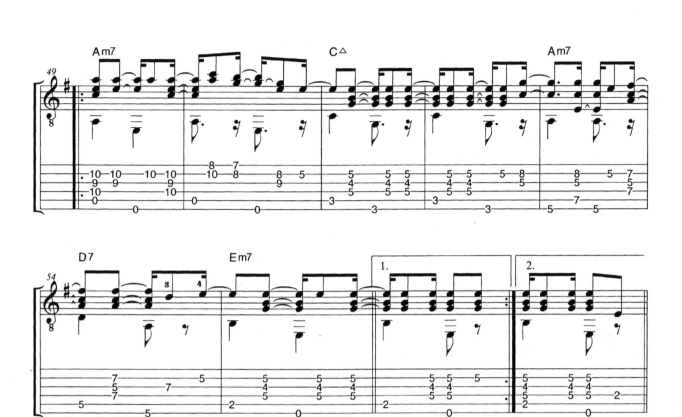

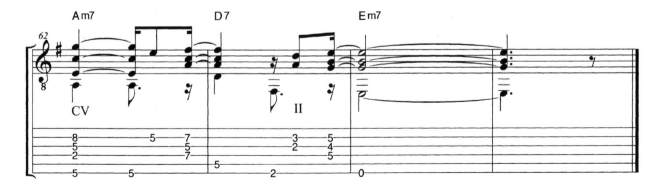

47

A Felicidade
(rhythm accomp. study)

words and music by
Vinicius De Moraes, Andre Salvet,
Antonio Carlos Jobim

arr. John Zaradin

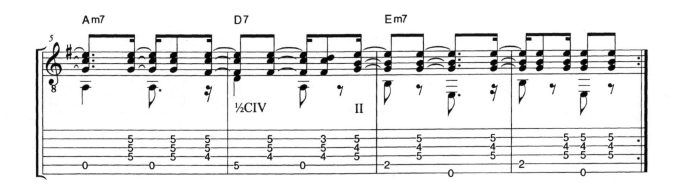

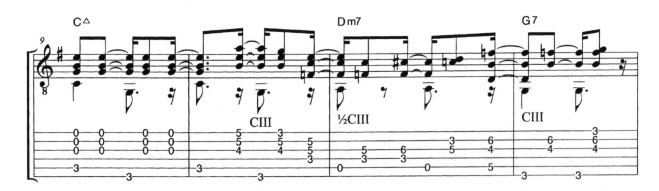

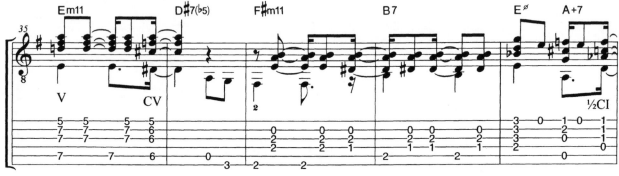

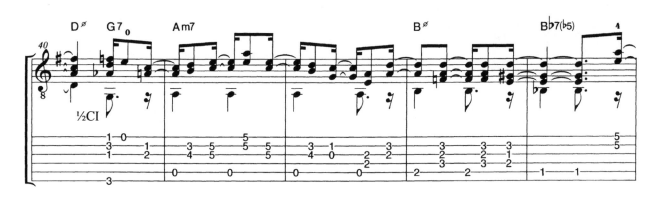

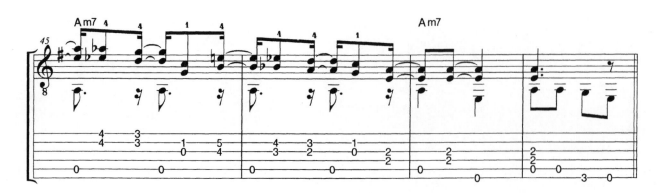

Gentle Rain

Medium Ballad / Bossa

music by Luiz Bonfa
words by Matt Dubey

one,_____ you have me_____ in the world,_____ and our love_____ will be

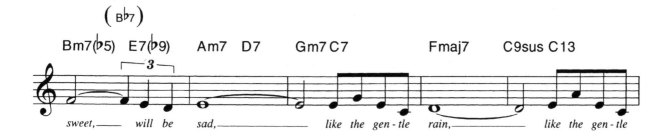

sweet,____ will be sad,_____ like the gen-tle rain,_____ like the gen-tle

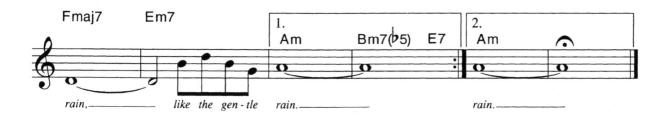

rain,_____ like the gen-tle rain._____ rain._____

Gentle Rain

(solo guitar)

arr. John Zaradin

music by Luiz Bonfa
words by Matt Dubey

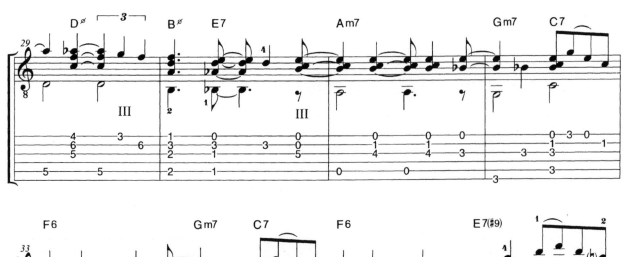

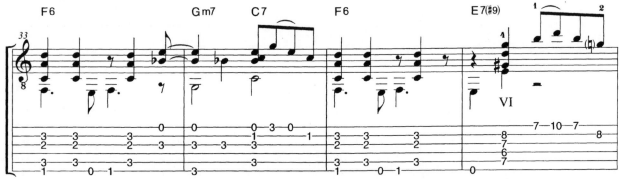

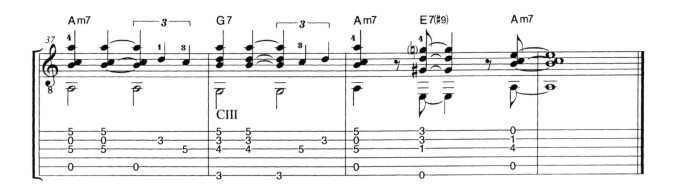

56

10

Gentle Rain

(rhythm accomp. study)

arr. John Zaradin

music by Luiz Bonfa
words by Matt Dubey

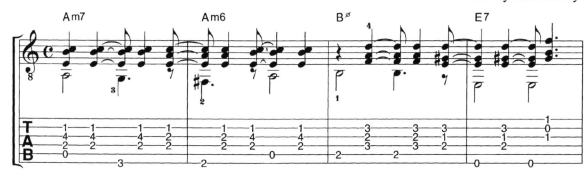

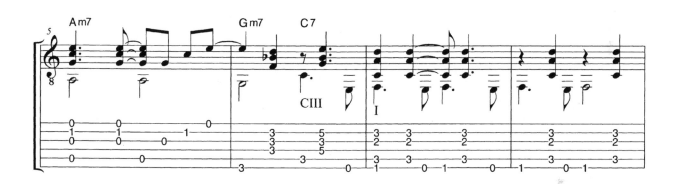

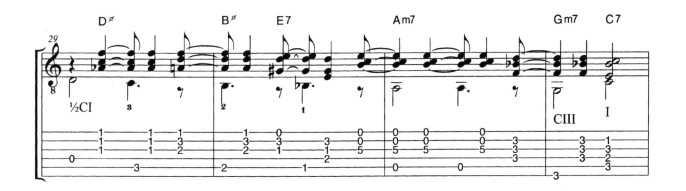

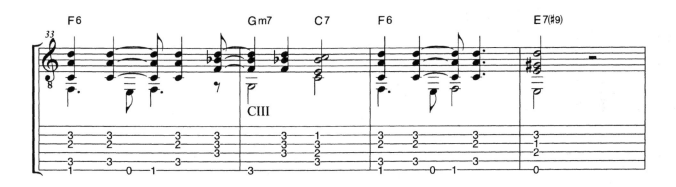

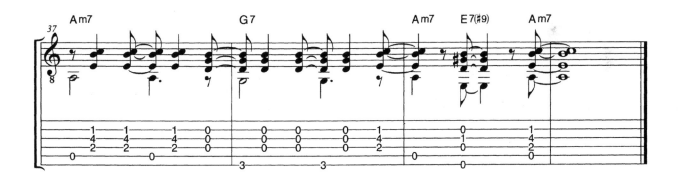

The Girl From
Ipanema

Bossa Nova

music by Antonio Carlos Jobim
original words by Vinicius De Moraes
English words by Norman Gimbel

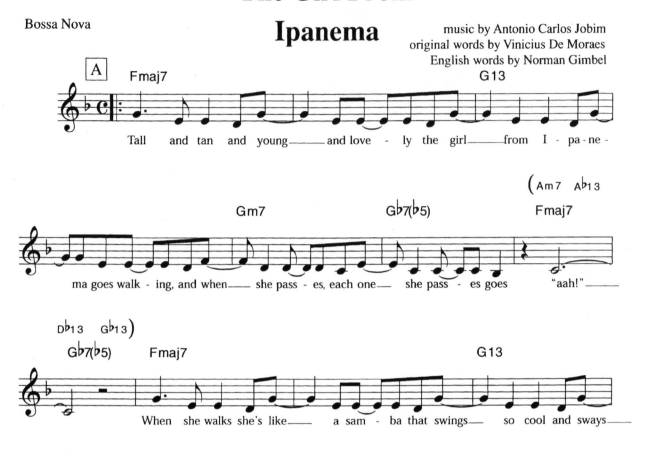

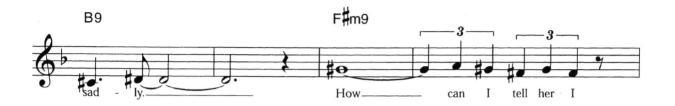

sad - ly. How can I tell her I

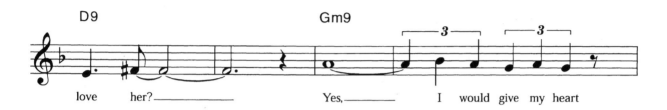

love her? Yes, I would give my heart

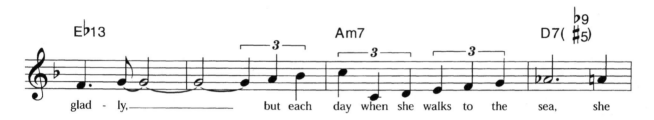

glad - ly, but each day when she walks to the sea, she

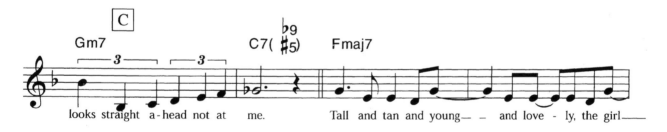

looks straight a-head not at me. Tall and tan and young— — and love - ly, the girl—

from I - pa - ne - ma goes walk - ing, and when— she pass - es I smile,.

— but she does-n't see. She just does-n't see. No, she does-n't see.

11

The Girl From Ipanema

(solo guitar)

arr. Mike Christiansen

music by Antonio Carlos Jobim
orig. words by Vinicius De Moraes
English words by Norman Gimbel

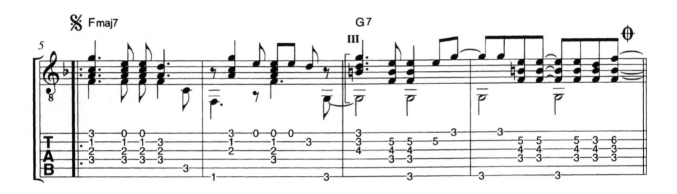

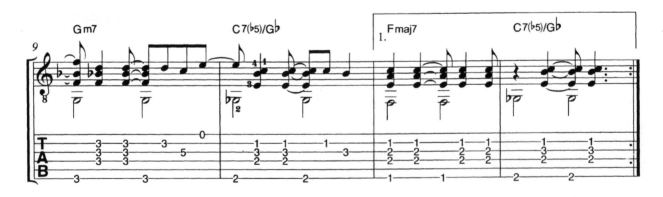

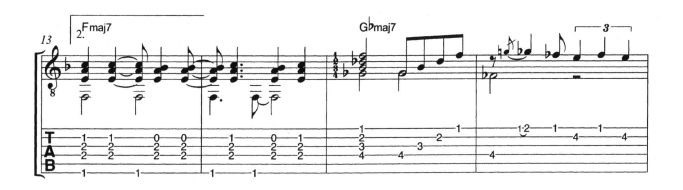

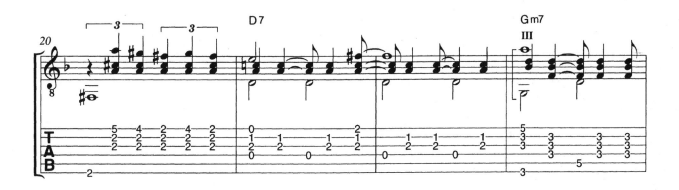

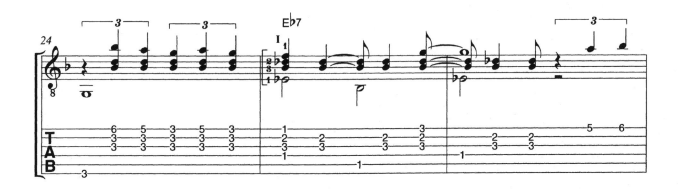

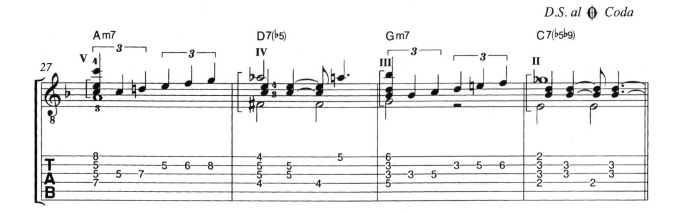

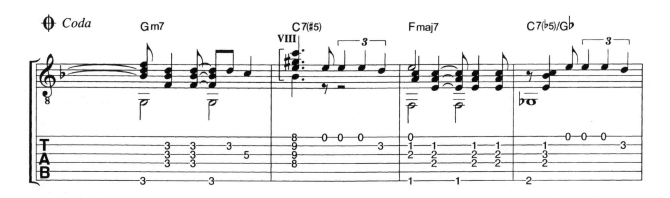

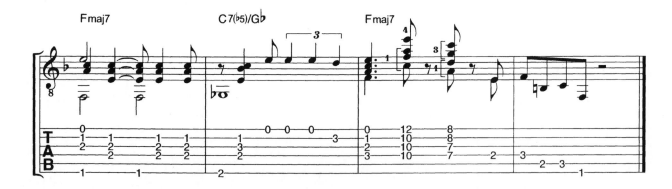

12

The Girl From Ipanema

(rhythm accomp. study)

arr. Mike Christiansen

music by Antonio Carlos Jobim
orig. words by Vinicius De Moraes
English words by Norman Gimbel

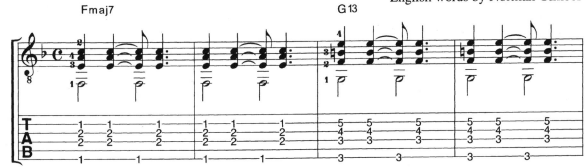

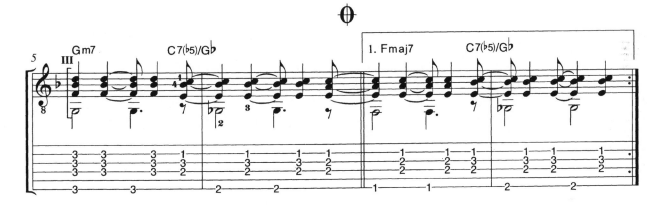

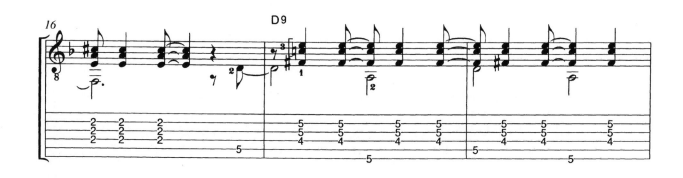

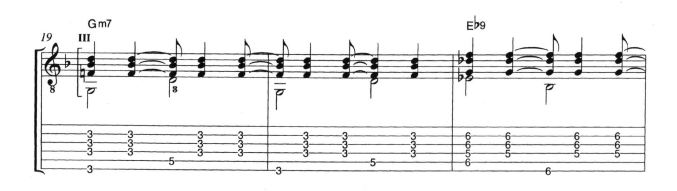

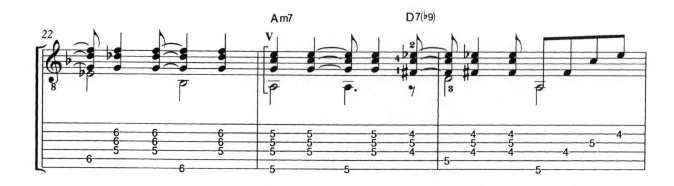

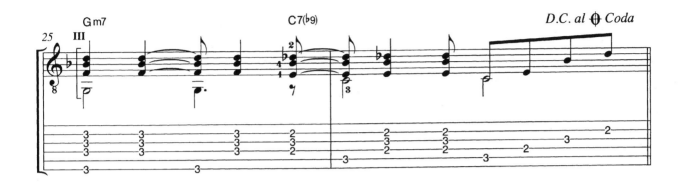

How Insensitive

music by Antonio Carlos Jobim
original words by Vinicius De Moraes
English words by Norman Gimbel

Bossa Nova

How Insensitive
(solo guitar)

arr. Mike Christiansen

music by Antonio Carlos Jobim
original words by Vinicius De Moraes
English words by Norman Gimbel

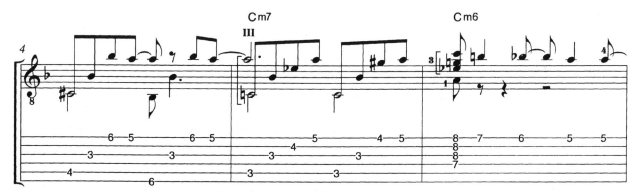

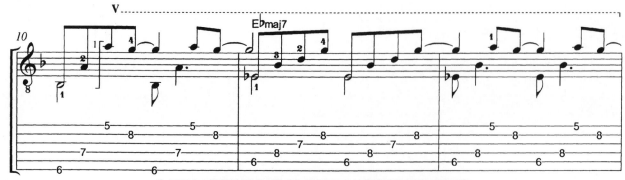

How Insensitive
(rhythm accomp. study)

music by Antonio Carlos Jobim
original words by Vinicius De Moraes
English words by Norman Gimbel

arr. Mike Christiansen

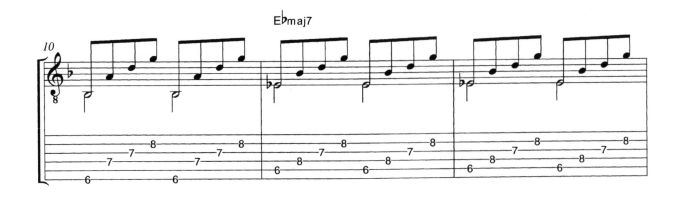

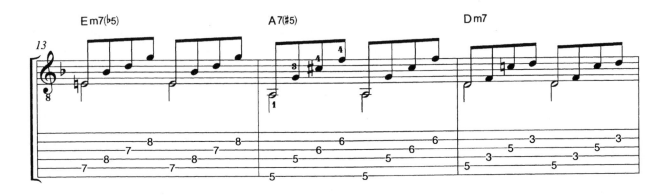

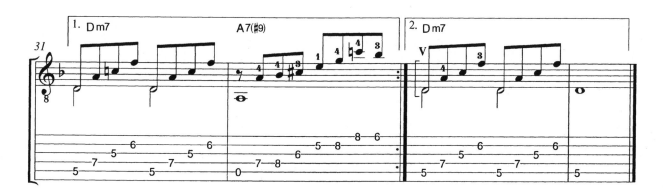

Meditation

music by Antonio Carlos Jobim
original words by Newton Mendonca
English words by Norman Gimbel

Bossa Nova Tempo

Intro

ta-ting how sweet— life will be——— when you come— back to me.———

D Optional Tag

15

Meditation
(solo guitar)

arr. Mike Christiansen

music by Antonio Carlos Jobim
orig. words by Newton Mendonca
English words by Norman Gimbel

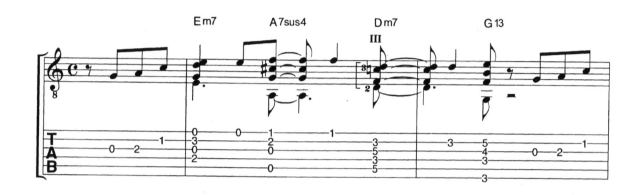

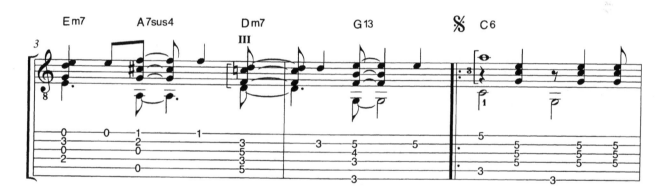

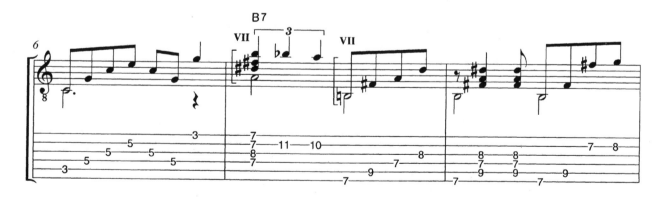

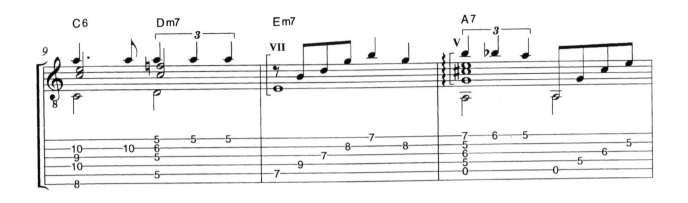

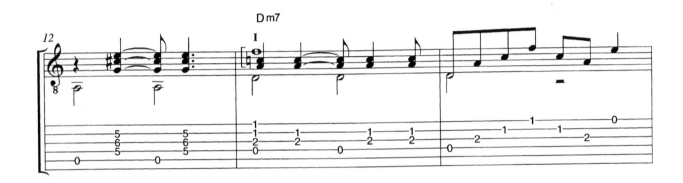

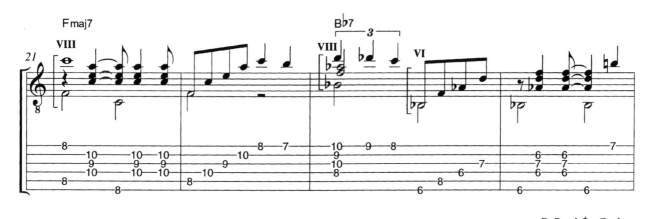

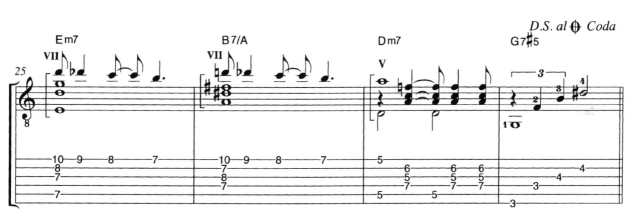

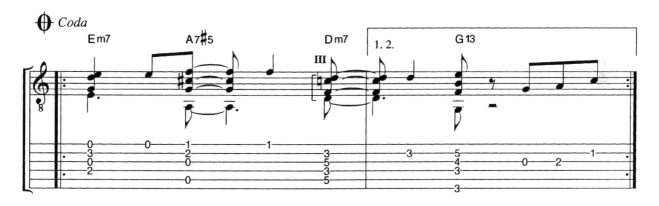

16

Meditation
(rhythm accomp. study)

music by Antonio Carlos Jobim
original words by Vinicius De Moraes
English words by Norman Gimbel

arr. Mike Christiansen

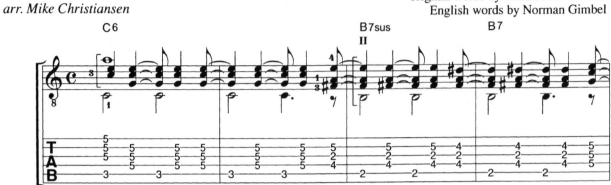

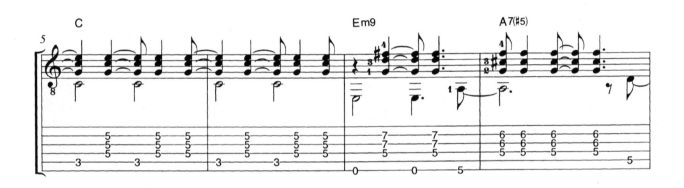

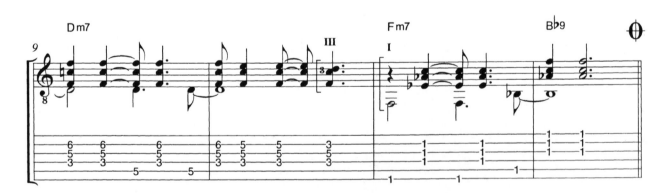

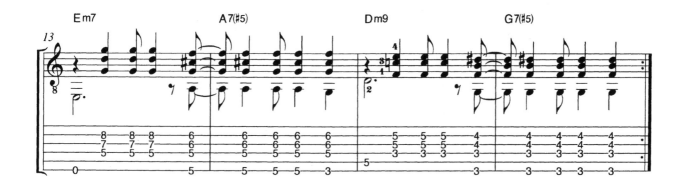

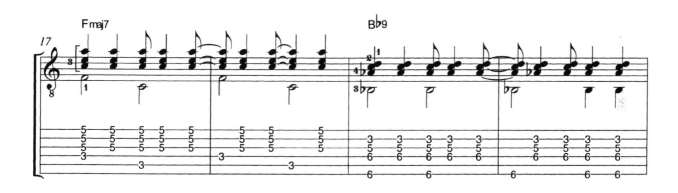

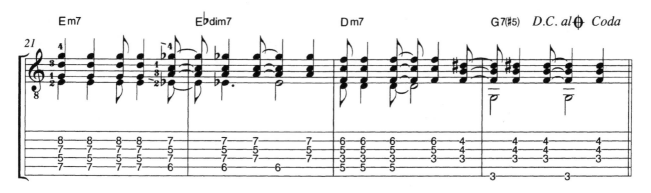

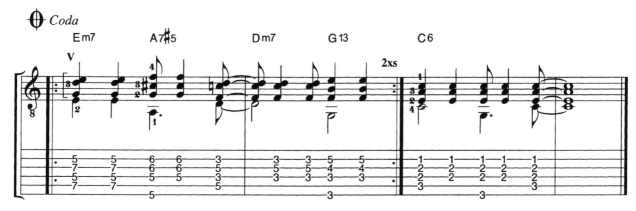

One Note Samba

music by Antonio Carlos Jobim
original words by Newton Mendonca
English words by Jon Hendricks

One Note Samba

(solo guitar)

music by Antonio Carlos Jobim
orig. words by Newton Mendonca
English words by Jon Hendricks

arr. Mike Christiansen

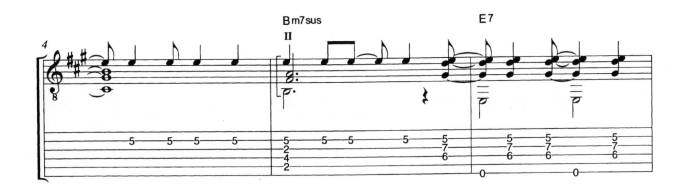

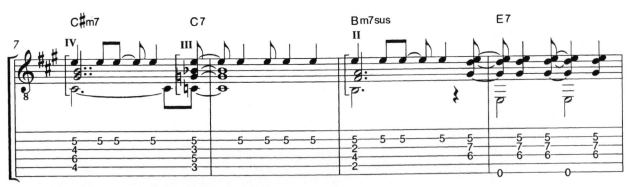

* To allow the use of open strings and facilitate certain chord voicings,
the key of this solo arrangement has been changed from the original.

87

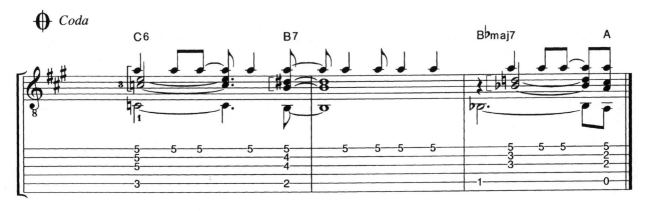

88

One Note Samba
(rhythm accomp. study)

music by Antonio Carlos Jobim
original words by Newton Mendonca
English words by Jon Hendricks

arr. Mike Christiansen

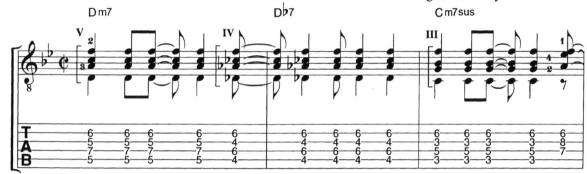

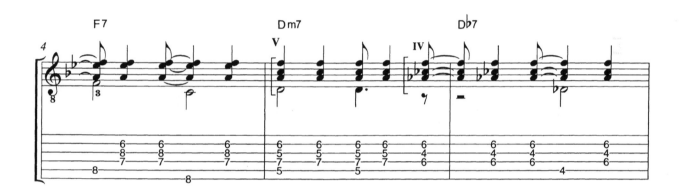

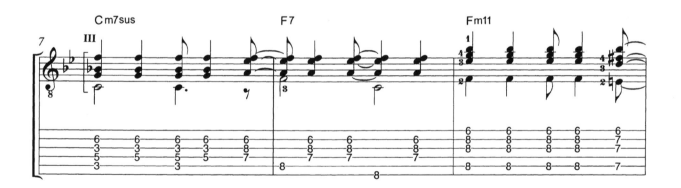

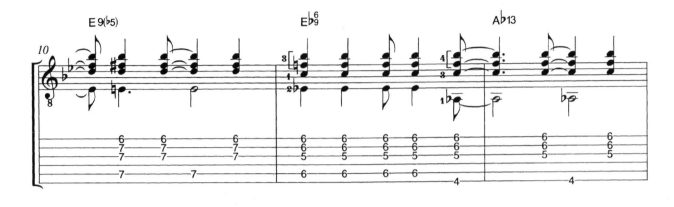

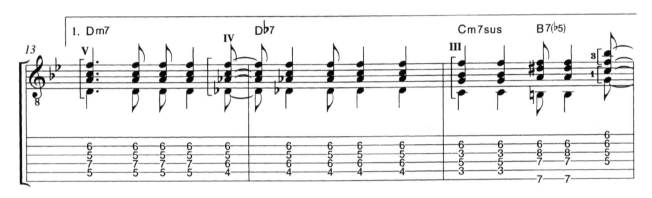

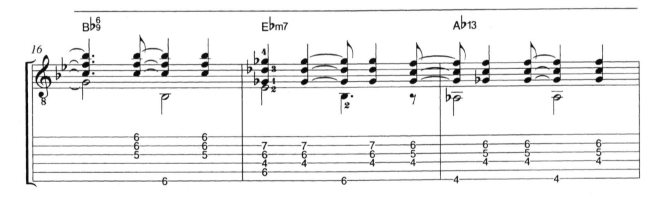

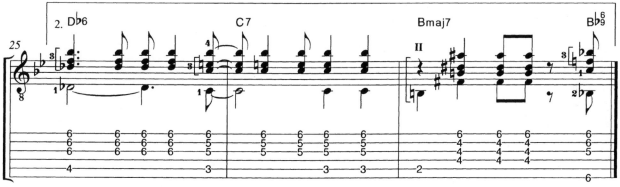

91

Quiet Nights of Quiet Stars

English Words by Gene Lees
original words and music by Antonio Carlos Jobim

Bossa Nova

A

Qui - et nights of qui - et stars,___ qui - et chords from my___

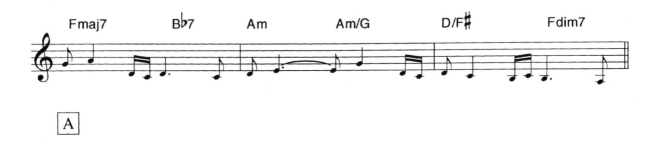

___ gui - tar___ float - ing on the si - lence that___ sur - rounds___

Fdim7   Fmaj7   Fm7

— us.—————————   Qui - et thoughts and qui -

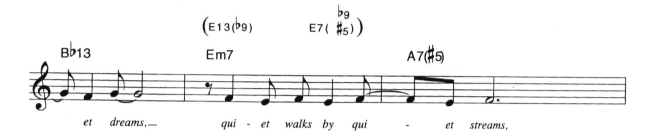

(E13(♭9)   E7(♭9♯5))

B♭13   Em7   A7(♯5)

et dreams,—   qui - et walks by qui - et streams,

D7   Dm7

and a win-dow look - ing on— the moun - tains and the sea.—

B

A♭dim7   D7/A

— How love - ly!   This is where I want— to be.—

A♭dim7   Gm7   ⌐3⌐

Here, with you so close— to me— un - til— the fin - al

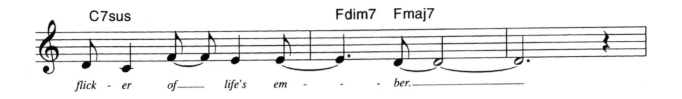

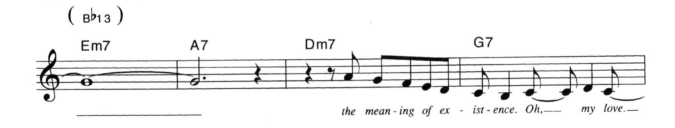

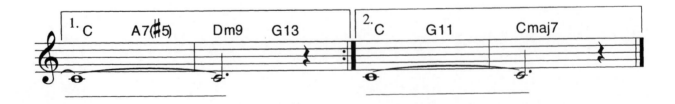

This page has been left blank
to avoid awkward page turns.

19

Quiet Nights of Quiet Stars

(solo guitar)

arr. Mike Christiansen

English words by Gene Lees
orig. words and music by Antonio Carlos Jobim

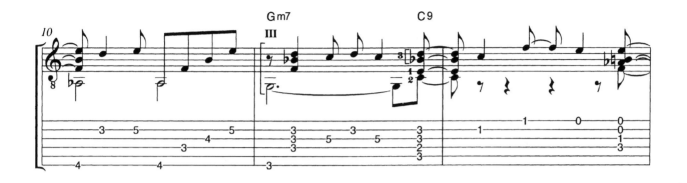

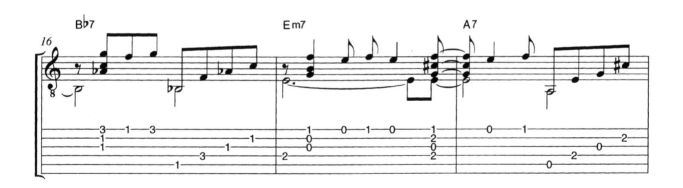

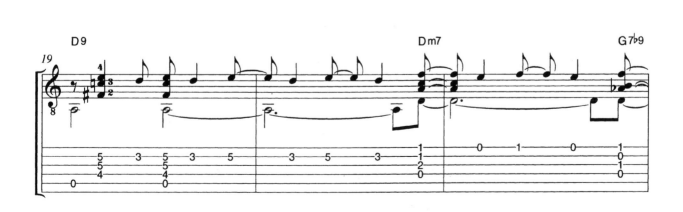

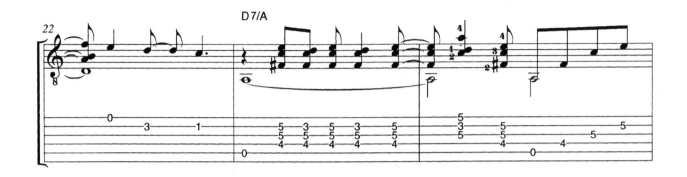

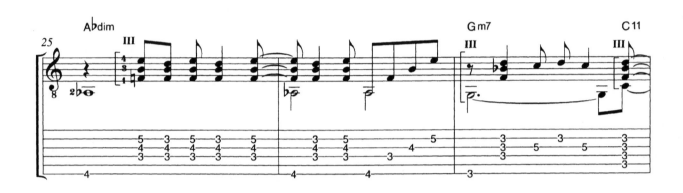

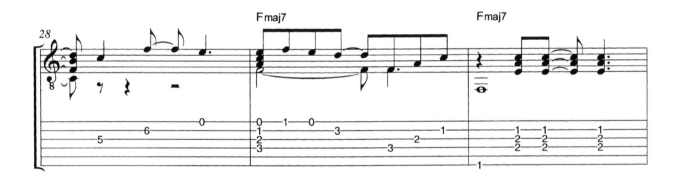

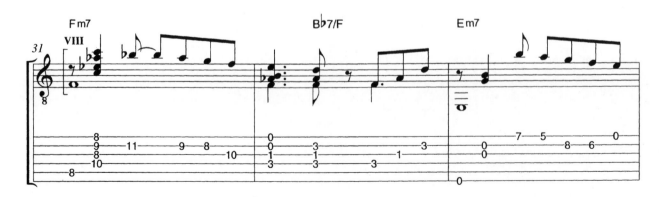

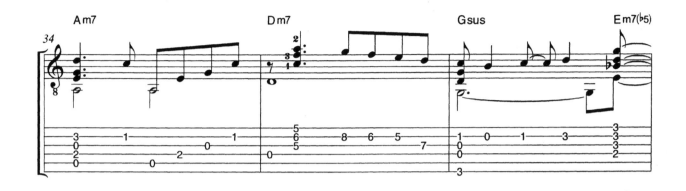

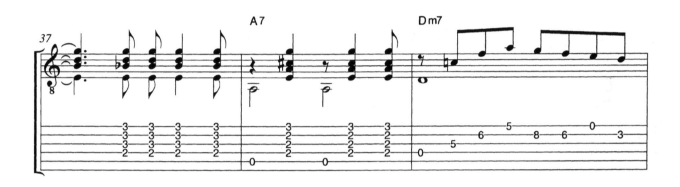

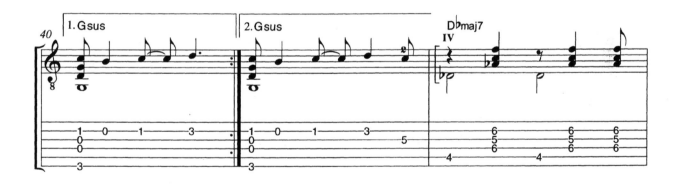

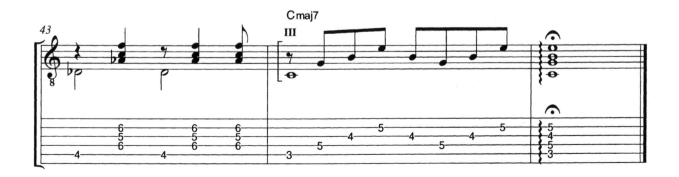

99

20

Quiet Nights of Quiet Stars

(rhythm accomp. study)

arr. Mike Christiansen

English words by Gene Lees
orig. words and music by Antonio Carlos Jobim

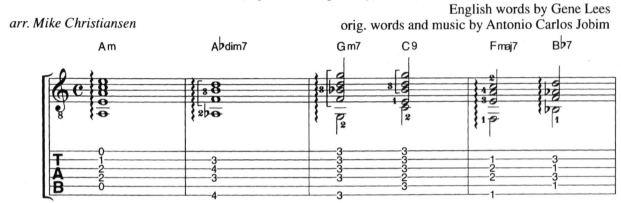

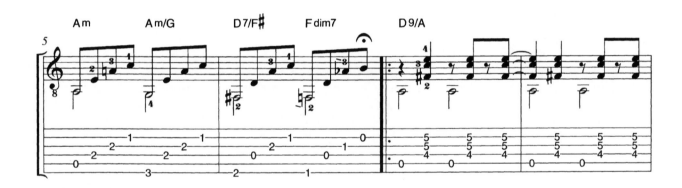

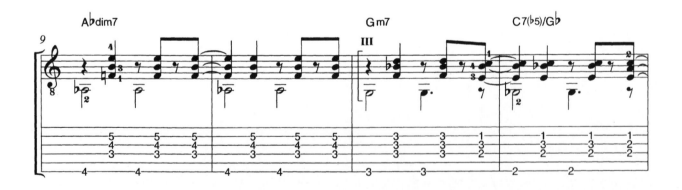

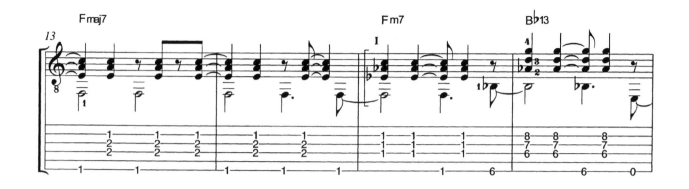

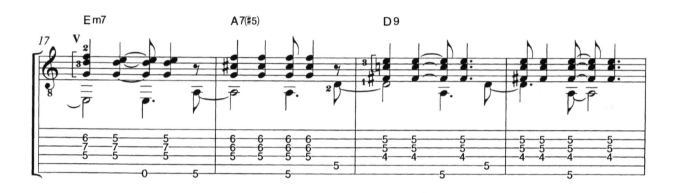

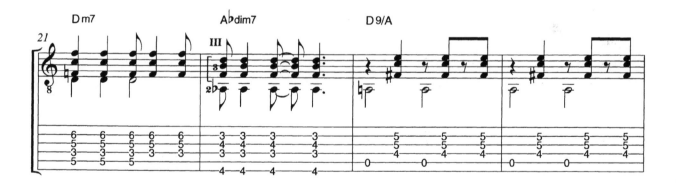

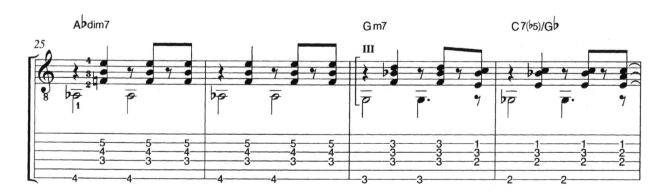

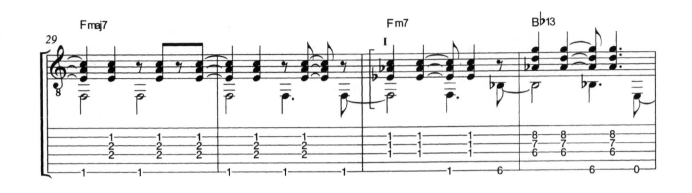

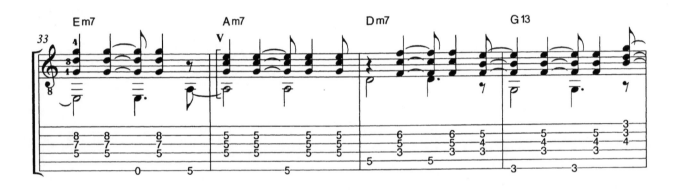

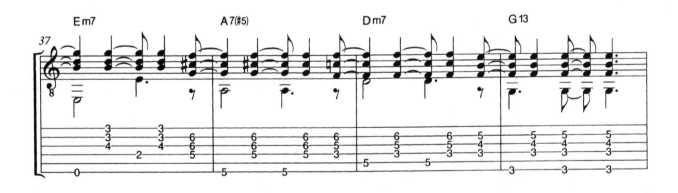

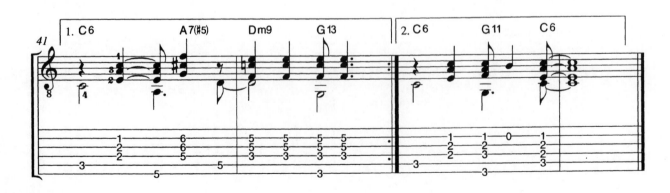

Sabia

music by Antonio Carlos Jobim
Portuguese lyric by Chico Buarque
English lyric by Norman Gimbel

Moderate Bossa

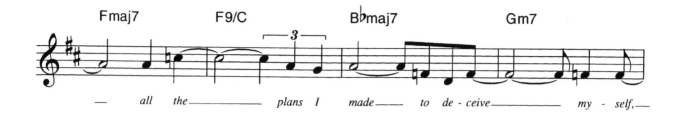

all the _____ plans I made _____ to de - ceive _____ my - self, _____

_____ all the roads _____ I made _____ just to lose _____ my - self, _____

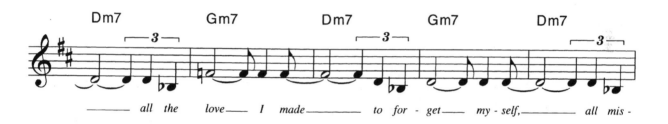

_____ all the love _____ I made _____ to for - get _____ my - self, _____ all mis -

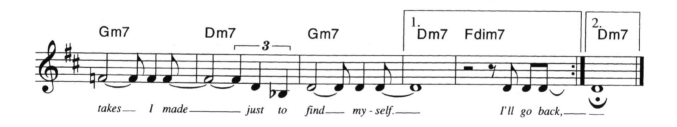

takes _____ I made _____ just to find _____ my - self. _____   I'll go back, _____

105

Sabía

(solo guitar)

arr. John Zaradin

music by Antonio Carlos Jobim
Portuguese lyric by Chico Buarque
English lyric by Norman Gimbel

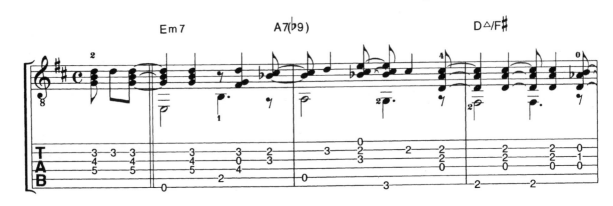

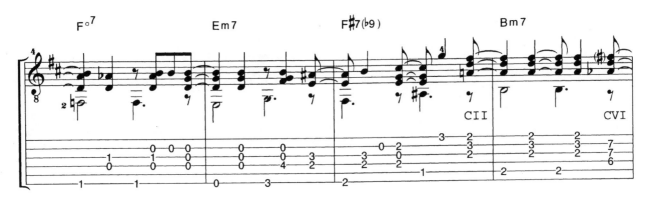

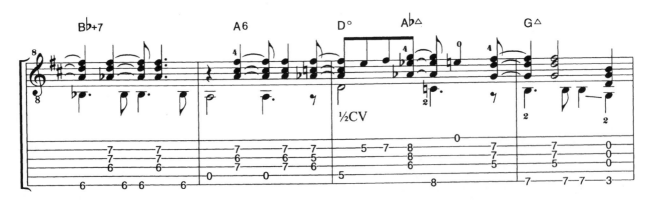

Sabía
(rhythm accomp. study)

arr. John Zaradin

music by Antonio Carlos Jobim
Portuguese lyric by Chico Buarque
English lyric by Norman Gimbel

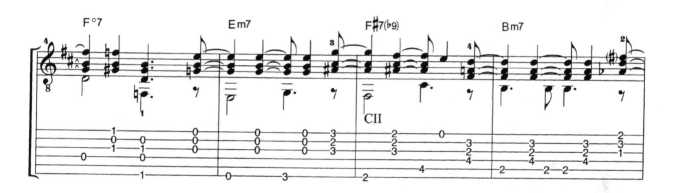

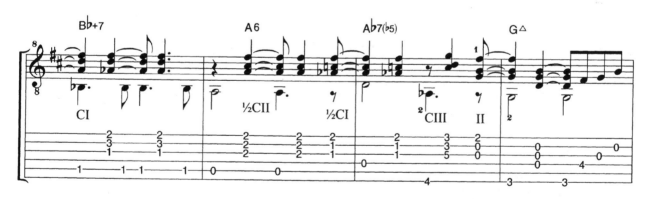

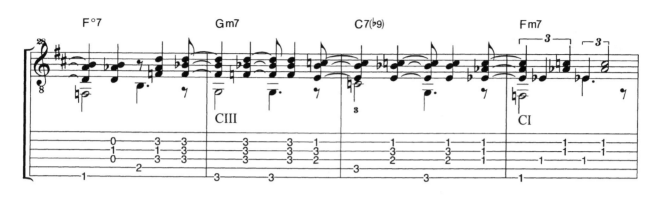

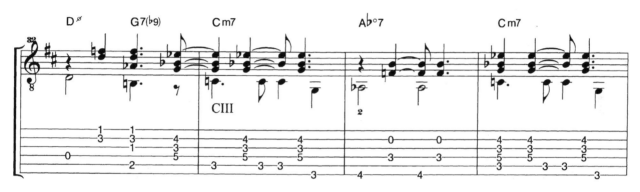

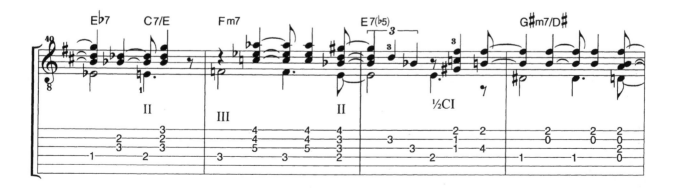

113

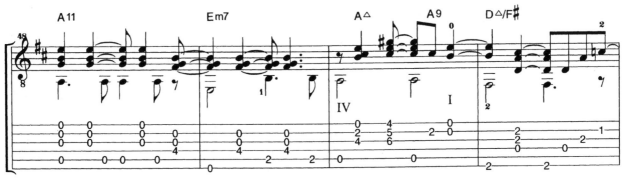

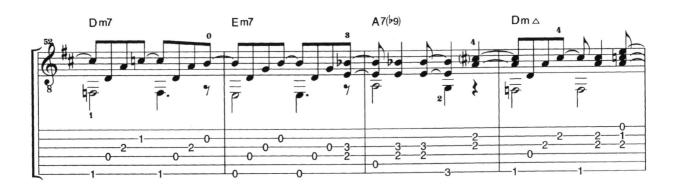

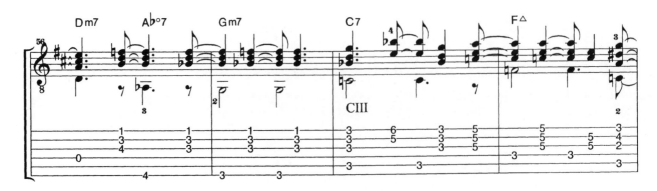

114

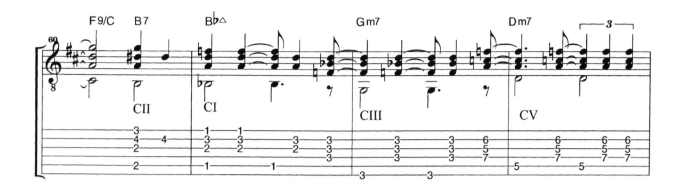

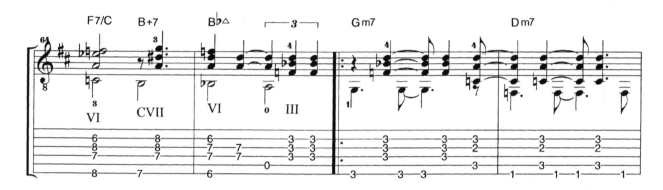

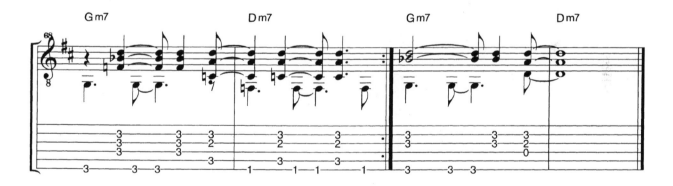

So Nice

(Summer Samba)

by Marcos Valle and Paulo Sergio Valle
(original words and music)
and Norman Gimbel (English words)

Medium Bossa

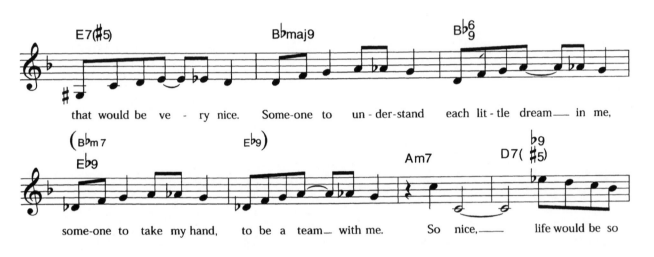

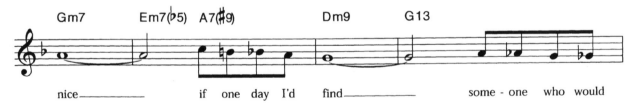

stay with me right——or wrong, some-one to sing to me some lit - tle sam - ba song.

Some-one to take my heart, then give his heart— to me. Some-one who's read - y to

give love a start— with me. Oh yes,——— that would be so nice.———

Should it be you and me, I could see that would be nice.

So Nice
(solo guitar)

arr. John Zaradin

original words and music
by Marcos Valle and Paulo Sergio Valle
English words byNorman Gimbel

119

So Nice

(rhythm accomp. study)

original words and music
by Marcos Valle and Paulo Sergio Valle
English words by Norman Gimbel

arr. John Zaradin

The Island
(Comecar De Novo)

by Alan and Marilyn Bergman,
Ivan Lins and Vitor Martins

Moderate Latin/Ballad

Make be - lieve ___ we've land ed - ___ on a des - ert is -
On our lit - tle is - land ___ not a soul ___ can see ___

land. Bathe me in ___ the wa - ters,
___ us; show me how ___ to love ___ you,

warm me in ___ the moon - light. Taste me with your
teach me how ___ to please ___ you. Lay your dreams be -

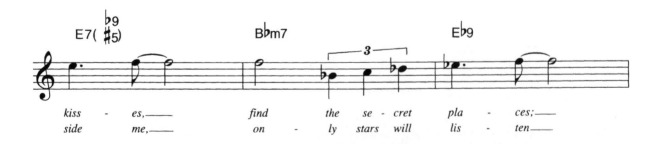

kiss - es, ___ find the se - cret pla - ces;
side me, ___ on - ly stars will lis - ten

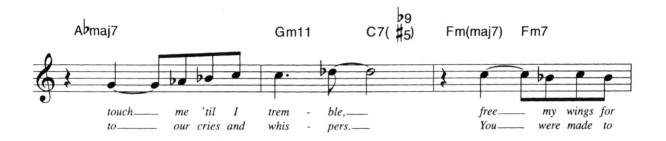

touch___ me 'til I trem - ble,___ free___ my wings for
to___ our cries and whis - pers. You___ were made to

fly - ing___ and catch me while I'm fall - - ing.___
love me___ and I was made to love___ you.___

* Vocal usually sung one octave lower.

Keep your arms a - round___ me___ like there's no to - mor -
Keep your arms a - round___ me; lose your - self in - side___

row.___ Let me know you love me.
— me,___

123

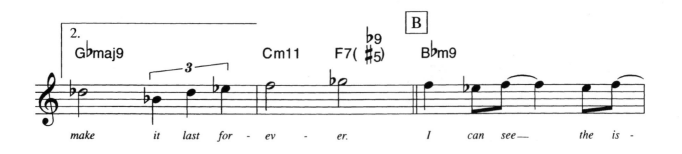

make it last for - ev - er. I can see— the is -

land shin - ing in— the dis - tance.

Now we're get - ting clos - er. Keep your arms a - round—

— me,——— love, we're al - most there!

rit.

This page has been left blank
to avoid awkward page turns.

The Island
(solo guitar)

arr. *John Zaradin*

by Alan and Marilyn Bergman,
Ivan Lins and Vitor Martins

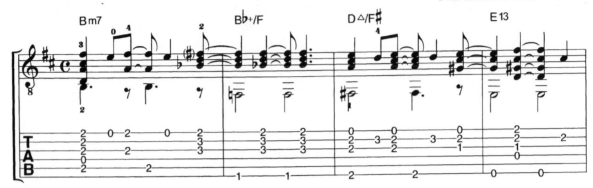

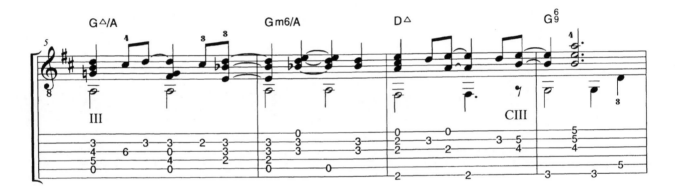

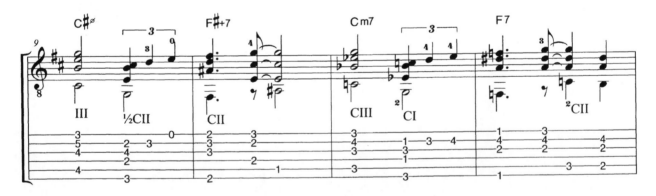

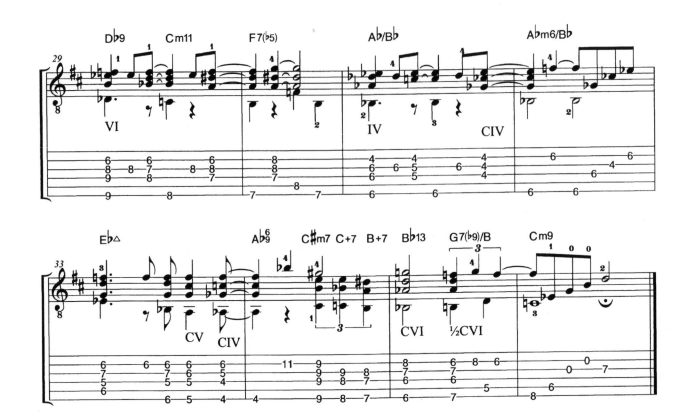

128

The Island

(rhythm accomp. study)

by Alan and Marilyn Bergman,
Ivan Lins and Vitor Martins

arr. John Zaradin

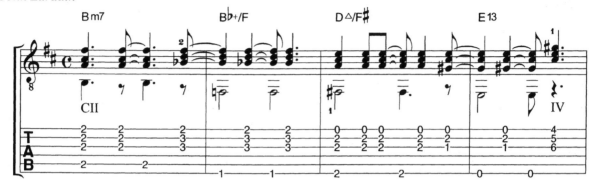

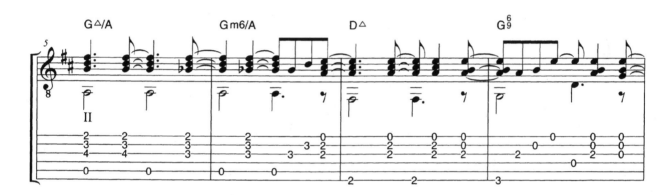

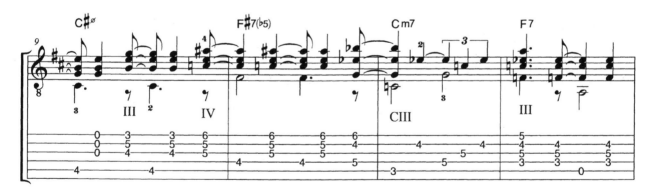

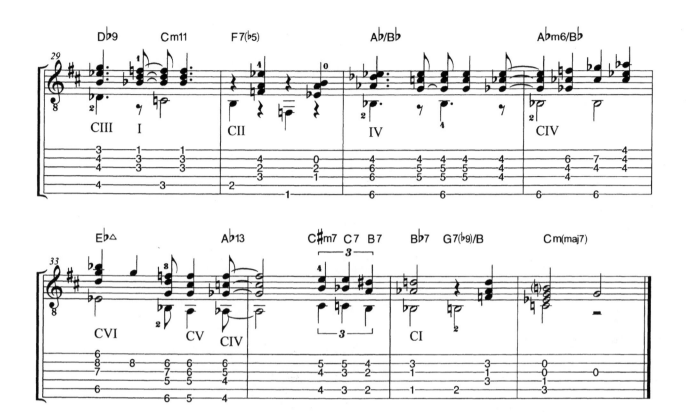

Mike Christiansen

Mike Christiansen is a Professor and Director of Guitar Studies at Utah State University. In 1994 he was selected "Professor of the Year" at Utah State. He is the author of numerous instructional books, has recorded several CDs, and appears on fourteen instructional videos. He has had articles published in several magazines including Acoustic Guitar and Soundboard, and has also conducted many workshops for guitarists and educators. In addition to this work geared toward teaching, he has played in many top bands and ensembles, has written and performed radio jingles, has backed up many artists on recordings and has written and recorded music for TV and educational films. Currently, in addition to his teaching and writing duties, Mike does solo work, performs with the Lightwood Duo (a clarinet-guitar duo), and many studio sessions.

John Zaradin

John Zaradin's professional life began performing with the violinist, Jan Resek, in
Germany and the UK, after which his London
debut concert, in 1968, at the Purcell Room,
Royal Festival Hall, launched him into the
London musical world. Here, he was exposed
to a wide variety of music and was called
upon to perform in studios, in theatre and on
the concert platform. He made, at this time,
with the London Symphony Orchestra, the
guitar recordings for the television series The
Strauss Family.

His London theatre life began at the Royal
Court Theatre with Shakespeare's Twelfth
Night (director Jane Howells), evolved onto
the West End stage at the Piccadilly Theatre
with *Man of La Mancha* and continued into
touring with the musicals *Hair* and *Fiddler on
the Roof* and with the companies Ballet
Rambert, London Contemporary Dance and
Glyndebourne Opera.

In 1972 Belwin Mills became his first publish-
er and he made his first solo recording
Concierto de Aranguez by J. Rodrigo of
(EMI/CFP). Later that year, he was invited to
join the Royal Shakespeare Company for the
world tour of his production of Midsummer
Night's Dream.

Returning to Europe, John toured as soloist, with Brazilian companies, presented his own group
Images of Brazil and recorded a second album *Zaradin's Guitar* for EMI (1976). This group Images of
Brazil, playing original compositions and a kaleidoscope of music from Brazil, made television and
radio performances and performed in venues, which ranged from Ronnie Scott's Jazz Club to the
Queen Elizabeth Hall, London.